Prais

"Don't let the size of this boo[k] ... doesn't have much to say ab[out] ... each sentence—is rich in insight, wisdom, compassion, and most of all, comfort. Ronald Rolheiser gently dismantles the age-old myths and taboos associated with suicide, and gives brokenhearted survivors of suicide loss genuine reasons for hope. The greatest gift Rolheiser gives to the reader is the reassurance that Christ can enter a heart that is locked in fear and wound, and that our bruised and wounded loved ones are 'in far gentler hands than our own.'"

—KAY WARREN,
cofounder of Saddleback Church, Lake Forest, California

ↄↄ

"With empathy and pastoral wisdom, this book provides unique insights on the nature of suicide, its devastating effects, and God's embracing love throughout. Fr. Ron is exactly who I would have wanted at my side when my daughter died."

—MARJORIE ANTUS,
author of *My Daughter, Her Suicide, and God: A Memoir of Hope*

ALSO BY RONALD ROLHEISER

Against an Infinite Horizon: The Finger of God in Our Everyday Lives

Forgotten Among the Lilies: Learning to Love Beyond Our Fears

Our One Great Act of Fidelity: Waiting for Christ in the Eucharist

Prayer: Our Deepest Longing

Sacred Fire: A Vision for a Deeper Human and Christian Maturity

Secularity and the Gospel: Being Missionaries to Our Children

The Holy Longing: Guidelines for a Christian Spirituality

The Passion and the Cross

The Restless Heart: Finding Our Spiritual Home in Times of Loneliness

The Shattered Lantern: Rediscovering a Felt Presence of God

BRUISED & WOUNDED

Struggling to Understand Suicide

∽

RONALD ROLHEISER

PARACLETE PRESS
BREWSTER, MASSACHUSETTS

2019 Second Printing
2018 First Printing

Bruised & Wounded: Struggling to Understand Suicide

Copyright © 2018 by Ronald Rolheiser

ISBN 978-1-64060-084-3

The Paraclete Press name and logo (dove on cross) are trademarks of
Paraclete Press, Inc.

Library of Congress Cataloging-in-Publication Data
Names: Rolheiser, Ronald, author.
Title: Bruised and wounded : struggling to understand suicide / Ronald
    Rolheiser.
Description: Brewster, Massachusetts : Paraclete Press Inc., 2017.
Identifiers: LCCN 2017051238 | ISBN 9781640600843 (trade paper)
Subjects: LCSH: Consolation. | Death–Religious aspects–Christianity. |
    Suicide–Religious aspects–Christianity. | Bereavement–Religious
    aspects–Christianity. | Grief–Religious aspects–Christianity.
Classification: LCC BV4909 .R65 2017 | DDC 248.8/66–dc23
LC record available at https://lccn.loc.gov/2017051238

10 9 8 7 6 5 4 3 2

Published by Paraclete Press
Brewster, Massachusetts
www.paracletepress.com

Printed in the United States of America

CONTENTS

INTRODUCTION 7

1 BRUISED AND WOUNDED 17

2 REMOVING THE TABOO 27

3 DESPAIR AS WEAKNESS
RATHER THAN SIN 47

4 RECLAIMING THE MEMORY
OF OUR LOVED ONE 53

5 THE PAIN OF THE ONES LEFT BEHIND 59

6 DYING INTO SAFE HANDS 69

INTRODUCTION

A friend of mine recently attended the funeral of a man who had taken his own life. At the end of the service the deceased man's brother spoke to the congregation. After highlighting his brother's generosity and sensitivity and sharing some anecdotes that helped celebrate his life, he went on to say something about the manner of his death. Here, in effect, are his words:

When someone is stricken with cancer, one of three things can happen: Sometimes doctors can treat the disease and, in essence, cure it. Sometimes the medical professionals cannot cure the disease but can control it enough so that the person suffering from cancer can live with the disease for the rest of his or her life. Sometimes, however, the cancer is of a kind that cannot be treated. All the medicine and treatments in the world are powerless, and the person dies.

Certain kinds of emotional depression work the same way: Sometimes they can be treated so that, in effect, the person is cured. Sometimes they cannot ever really be cured, but they can be treated in such a way that the person can live with the disease for his or her whole life. And sometimes, just as with certain kinds of cancer, the disease is untreatable, unstoppable; no intervention by anyone or anything can halt its advance. Eventually it kills the person, and there is nothing anyone can do. My brother's depression was of that kind, the terminal kind.

This can be helpful, I believe, for any of us who have suffered the loss of a loved one to suicide.

All death unsettles us, but suicide leaves us with a very particular series of emotional, moral, and religious scars. It brings with it an ache, a chaos, a darkness, and a stigma that has to be experienced to be believed. Sometimes we deny it, but it's always there, irrespective of our religious and moral beliefs. Indeed, as part of its darkness and stigma, suicide not only takes our loved ones away from us, but it also takes away our true memory of them. The gift that they brought into our lives is now no longer celebrated. We never again speak with pride about their lives. Their pictures come off the wall, photos of them get buried deep inside drawers that we never open again, their names are less and less mentioned in conversation, and of the manner of their death we rarely speak. Suicide takes our loved ones away from us in more ways than we sometimes admit.

And there is no easy answer for how to reverse that, though a better understanding of suicide can be a start.

Not all suicides are of the same kind. Some suicides come about because the person is too arrogant and too hard of heart to want to live in this world. But that, I submit, is the exception, not the norm. Most suicides, certainly all the cases that I have known, come about for the opposite reason—namely, the person is too bruised and oversensitive to have the resiliency needed to continue to cope with life. In these cases, and that is the vast majority of suicides, the cause of death can pretty accurately be termed as cancer, emotional cancer. Just as with physical cancer, the person dying of suicide is taken out of this life against his or her will. Death by suicide is the emotional equivalent of cancer, a stroke, or a heart attack. Thus, its patterns are the same as those of cancer, strokes, and heart attacks. Death can happen suddenly, or it can be the end product of a long struggle that slowly wears a person down. Either way, it's involuntary.

As human beings, we are neither pure angels nor pure animals, but we are always both body and soul, one psychosomatic whole. And either part can break down.

This can be helpful in understanding suicide, though a better understanding will not necessarily mean that the darkness and stigma that surround it will simply go away. We will still feel many of the same things we felt before in the face of suicide: We will still feel awful. We will still feel conflicted and be given over to guilt feelings and second-guessing. We will still feel uneasy about how this person died and will still feel a certain dis-ease in talking about the manner of his or her death. We will still feel a certain hesitancy in celebrating that person's life in the manner we would have had the death been by natural causes. We will still go to our own graves with a black hole in our hearts. The pain of a suicide leaves its own indelible mark on the soul.

But at a different level of understanding something else will break through that will help us better deal with all those conflicted feelings, —namely, empathy for and understanding of someone whose emotional immune system has broken down. And that understanding will also bring with it the concomitant consolation that God's empathy and understanding far exceeds our own.

Love Through Locked Doors

Some years ago, some other friends of mine lost a daughter to suicide. She was in her early twenties and had a history of clinical depression. An initial attempt at suicide failed. The family then rushed round her, brought her to the best doctors and psychiatrists, and generally tried in every way to love and coax her out of her depression. Nothing worked. Eventually she died by suicide. Looking at their efforts and the incapacity of their love to break through and save her life, we see how helpless human love can be at a point. Sometimes all our best efforts, patience, and affection can't break through to a frightened, depressed person.

In spite of everything, that person remains locked inside of herself, huddled in fear, inaccessible, bent upon self-destruction. All love, it seems, is powerless to penetrate.

Fortunately, we are not without hope. The redeeming love of God can do what we can't. God's love is not stymied in the same way as is ours. Unlike our own, it can go through locked doors and enter closed, frightened, bruised, lonely places and breathe out peace, freedom, and new life there. Our belief in this is expressed in one of the articles of the creed: *He descended into hell.*

What is meant by that? God descended into hell? Generally, we take this to mean that, between his death and resurrection, Jesus descended into some kind of hell or limbo wherein lived the souls of all the good persons who had died since the time of Adam. Once there, Jesus took them all with him to heaven. More recently, some theologians have taken this article of faith to mean that, in his death, Jesus experienced alienation from his Father and thus experienced in some real sense the pain of hell. There is merit to these interpretations, but this doctrine also means something more. To say that Christ descended into hell is to, first and foremost, say something about God's love for us and how that love will go to any length, descend to any depth, and go through any barrier in order to embrace a wounded, huddled, frightened, and bruised soul. By dying as he did, Jesus showed that he loves us in such a way that his love can penetrate even our private hells, going right through the barriers of hurt, anger, fear, and hopelessness.

We see this expressed in an image in John's Gospel where, twice, Jesus goes right through locked doors, stands in the middle of a huddled circle of fear, and breathes out peace. That image of Jesus going through locked doors is surely the most consoling thought within the entire Christian faith (and is unrivalled in any other world religion). Simply put, it means that God can help us even when we can't help ourselves.

God can empower us even when we are too hurt, frightened, sick, and weak to even, minimally, help ourselves.

I remember a haunting, holy picture that I was given as a child. It showed a man, huddled in depression, in a dark room, behind a closed door. Outside stood Jesus, with a lantern, knocking softly on the door. The door only had a knob on its inside. Everything about the picture said: "Only you can open that door." Ultimately what is said in that picture is untrue. Christ doesn't need a doorknob. He can, and does, enter through locked doors. He can enter a heart that is locked up in fear and woundedness. What the picture says is true about human love. It can only knock and remain outside when it meets a heart that is huddled in fear and loneliness.

But that is not the case with God's love, as John 20 and our doctrine about the descent into hell make clear. God's love can, and does, descend into hell. It does not require that a wounded, emotionally paralyzed person first finds the strength to open herself to love. There is no private hell, no depression, no sickness, no fear, and even no bitterness so deep or so enclosed that God's love cannot descend into it. There are no locked doors through which Christ cannot go.

I am sure that when that young woman, whose suicide I mentioned earlier, awoke on the other side, Jesus stood inside of her huddled fear and spoke to her, softly and gently, those same words he spoke to his disciples on that first Easter day when he went through the locked doors behind which they were huddled and said: "Peace be with you! Again, I say it, Peace be with you!"

1
BRUISED AND WOUNDED

ℭ

The poet Hafiz wrote a poem nearly seven hundred years ago entitled, "We Should Talk About This Problem." In that poem, God addresses a wounded soul:

> There is a Beautiful Creature
> Living in a hole you have dug. . .
> And I often sing, but still, my dear,
> You do not come out.
> I have fallen in love with Someone
> Who hides inside of you.

That's God's feeling, and perhaps ours too, when someone is in a suicidal depression. Few things can so devastate us as the suicide of a loved one. There's the horrific shock of losing a loved one so suddenly that, just of itself, can bring us to our knees; but, with suicide, there are other soul-wrenching feelings too: confusion, guilt, second-guessing, religious anxiety. Where did we fail this person? What might we still have done? What is this person's state with God?

What needs to be said about this? First, that suicide is a disease and generally the most misunderstood of all sicknesses. It takes a person out of life against his or her will, the emotional equivalent of cancer, a stroke, or a heart attack. Second, we, those left behind, need not spend undue energy second-guessing as to how we might have failed that person, what we should have noticed, and what we might have done to prevent the suicide. Suicide is an illness and, as with any sickness, we can love someone and still not be able to save that person from death. God loved this person, too, and like us could not, this side of eternity, do anything either. Finally, we shouldn't worry too much about how God meets this person on the other side. God's love, unlike ours, can go through locked doors and touch what will not allow itself to be touched by us.

Is this making light of suicide? No. Anyone who has ever dealt with either the victim of a suicide before his or her death or with those grieving that death afterward knows that it is impossible to make light of it. There is no pain like the one suicide inflicts. Nobody who is healthy wants to die, and nobody who is healthy seeks to burden his or her loved ones with this kind of pain. And that's the point: This is only done when someone isn't healthy. The fact that medication can often prevent suicide should tell us something.

Suicide, in most cases, is an illness, not a sin. Nobody, who is healthy, willingly decides to die by suicide and burden his or her loved ones with that death any more than anyone willingly chooses to die of cancer and cause pain. The victim of suicide (in most cases) is a trapped person, caught up in a fiery, private chaos that has its roots both in his or her psyche and in his or her biochemistry. Suicide, in most cases, is a desperate attempt to end unendurable pain, akin to one throwing oneself off a high building because one's clothing is on fire.

Many of us have known victims of suicide, and we know, too, that in almost every case that person was not full of pride, haughtiness, and the desire to hurt anyone. Generally, it's the opposite. The victim has cancerous problems precisely because he or she is wounded, raw, and too bruised to have the resiliency needed to deal with life. Those of us who have lost loved ones to suicide know that the problem is not one of strength but of weakness— the person is too bruised to be touched.

I remember a comment I over heard at a funeral for a suicide victim. The priest had preached badly, hinting that this suicide was somehow the man's own fault and that suicide is always the ulti-mate act of despair. At the reception afterward, a neighbor of the victim expressed his displeasure at the priest's homily: "There are a lot of people in this world who should kill themselves," he lamented, "but those kind never do! This man is the last person who should have killed himself, because he was one of the most sensitive people I've ever met!" A book could be written on that statement. Too often it's the meek who seemingly lose the battle in this world.

Finally, we shouldn't worry too much about how God meets our loved ones who have fallen victim to suicide. God, as Jesus assures us, has a special affection for those of us who are too bruised and wounded to be touched. Jesus assures us, too, that God's love can go through locked doors and into broken places and free up what's paralyzed and help that which can no longer help itself. God is not blocked when we are. God can reach through.

And so our loved ones who have fallen victim to suicide are now inside of God's embrace, enjoying a freedom they could never quite enjoy here and being healed through a touch that they could never quite accept from us.

Nothing More Painful

There is perhaps nothing more painful in the world than for us to lose a loved one to suicide.

A couple of months ago, I received a letter from a woman, a mother, who had recently lost her twenty-eight-year-old son in this manner. The young man had been suffering from clinical depression for nearly eight years when he took his own life.

Her letter to me betrayed a healthy understanding (at some deep level) of what had happened as well as all the unhealthy fear and second-guessing we all have when we are confronted with the suicide of a loved one.

She recognized that his death was, in the end, due to illness (not to malice or weakness), that he had a gentle soul, and that God understands. She shared the intuition that her son is now in heaven.

At the same time, she worried, as we all do, whether her son had now found peace and where, if anywhere, she had failed him. She also worried that her faith was not strong enough, because it was not giving her the type of consolation that she felt it should. Her pain is deep—but it is also wide.

Thousands of parents and families and friends of suicide victims around the world are enduring similar pain.

There are, as for all the great mysteries of life, no definitive answers that dissolve all pain and questioning. But there are some important perspectives of which we must never lose sight.

First of all, at this time in our history, for all kinds of reasons, suicide is still perhaps the most misunderstood of all deaths. We still tend to think that because it is self-inflicted it is voluntary in a way that death through physical illness or accident is not.

As I have said, for most suicides, this is not true. A person dying of suicide dies, as does the victim of physical illness or accident, against his or her will. People die from physical heart attacks, strokes, cancer, HIV/AIDS, and accidents. Death by suicide is the same, except that we are dealing with an emotional heart attack, an emotional stroke, emotional HIV/AIDS, emotional cancer, and an emotional fatality.

This comparison is not an analogy. These two kinds of heart attacks, strokes, cancers, and accidents are indeed identical. In neither case is the person responsible for his or her own death, nor does the person leave this world of his or her own will.

Second, in most cases, we should not worry about the victim's eternal salvation. God is infinitely more understanding than we are, and God's hands are infinitely more gentle than ours. Imagine a loving mother, having just given birth, welcoming her child onto her breast for the first time, and then you will have some image of how the suicide victim is received into the next life.

Again, this is not an analogy. God is infinitely more gentle, loving, understanding and motherly than even the most perfect mother on earth. We need not worry much when an honest, over-sensitive, gentle, overwrought and emotionally crushed person leaves this world—even if that exit was far from ideal.

However, even given that truth, we should not expect that our faith will take away all the pain of losing a loved one through suicide. Faith is not meant to take the pain away, but rather to precisely give us the sense that the one we lost is in far gentler hands than our own and is now, after so much pain, finally at peace. Faith gives us insight but does not, of itself, take away the pain of loss and death.

Finally, we the living who loved that person must refrain from second-guessing ourselves with every kind of haunting question: What else might I have done? Where did I let this person down? If only I had been there. What if . . .?

We are human beings, not God. People die of illnesses and accidents all the time, and all the love and attentiveness in the world sometimes cannot prevent death. With suicide, we must recognize that we are dealing with an illness that, like cancer or heart disease, can be terminal irrespective of every human effort to restore health. There are sicknesses that no humans can cure.

We can grieve our inadequacy as humans, but we are not God. Ultimately, we must take consolation in the fact that we loved as best we could and that we have not really lost this person. He or she went back to God.

Our job now is not to second-guess, but to trust—trust that God is far more gentle and understanding than we are and that God, who is adequate, can give this person a peace that we never could.

2
REMOVING THE TABOO

☙

Suicide hits us so hard because it is surrounded with the ultimate taboo. In the popular mind, suicide is generally seen, consciously or unconsciously, as the ultimate act of despair, the ultimate bad thing a person can do. This shouldn't surprise us, since suicide does go against the deepest instinct inside us, our will to live. Thus, even when it's treated with understanding and compassion, it still leaves those left behind with a certain amount of shame and a lot of second-guessing. Also, more often than not, it ruins our memory of the person who died. Just as his or her photographs slowly disappear from our walls, the manner of his or her death is usually spoken about with an all-too-hushed discretion.

None of this should be surprising: Suicide is the ultimate taboo.

So what's to be said about suicide? How can we move toward understanding it more empathically? I have said some of this already, and it bears repeating. This is so important.

Understanding suicide more compassionately won't take away its sting—nothing will, except time—but our own long-term healing and the redemption of the memory of the one who died can be helped by keeping a number of things in mind.

- Suicide, in most cases, is a disease, not something freely willed. The person who dies in this way dies against his or her will, akin to those who jumped to their deaths from the Twin Towers after terrorist planes had set those buildings on fire on September 11, 2001. They were jumping to certain death, but only because they were already burning to death where they were standing. No one would suggest that they had lost the desire to live. Death by suicide is analogous to death by cancer, stroke, or a heart attack—except, in the case of suicide, it's a question of emotional cancer, emotional stroke, or an emotional heart attack. Moreover, still to be more fully explored, is the potential role that biochemistry plays in suicide. Since some suicidal depressions are treatable by drugs, clearly then some suicides are caused by biochemical deficiencies, as are many other diseases that kill us.

- The person who dies in this way, almost invariably, is a very sensitive human being. Suicide is rarely done in arrogance, as an act of contempt. There are of course examples of persons, like Hitler, who are too proud to endure normal human contingency and kill themselves out of arrogance, but that's a very different kind of suicide, not the kind that most of us have seen in a loved one. Generally, our own experience with the loved ones that we've lost to suicide was that these persons were anything but arrogant. More accurately described, they were too bruised to touch and were wounded in some deep way that we couldn't comprehend or help heal. Indeed, oftentimes when sufficient time has passed after their deaths, in retrospect, we get some sense of their wound, one which we never clearly perceived while they were alive. Their suicide then no longer seems as surprising.

- Finally, we need not worry unduly about the eternal salvation of those who die in this way. God's understanding and compassion infinitely surpass our own. Our lost loved ones are in safer hands than ours. If we, limited as we are, can already reach through this tragedy with some understanding and love, we can rest secure in the fact that, given the width and depth of God's love, the one who dies through suicide meets, on the other side, a compassion that's deeper than our own and a judgment that intuits the deepest motives of his or her heart.

Moreover, God's love, as we are assured of in our Scriptures and as is manifest in Jesus's resurrection, is not as helpless as our own in dealing with this. We, in dealing with our loved ones, sometimes find ourselves helpless, without a strategy and without energy, standing outside an oak-like door, shut out because of someone's fear, woundedness, sickness, or loneliness. Most persons who die by suicide are precisely locked inside this kind of private room by some cancerous wound through which we cannot reach and through which they themselves cannot reach. Our best efforts leave us still unable to penetrate that private hell. But, as we see in the resurrection appearances of Jesus, God's love and compassion are not rendered helpless by locked doors. God's love doesn't stand outside, helplessly knocking. Rather it goes right through the locked doors, stands inside the huddle of fear and loneliness, and breathes out peace. So too for our loved ones who die by suicide. We find ourselves helpless, but God can, and does, go through those locked doors and, once there, breathes out peace inside a tortured, huddled heart.

The Stigma of Suicide

Recently I read, in succession, three books on suicide, each written by a mother who lost one of her children to suicide. All three books are powerful, mature, not given to false sentiment, and worth reading: Lois Severson, who wrote *Healing the Wound from My Daughter's Suicide: Grief Translated into Words*, lost her daughter, Patty, to suicide; Gloria Hutchinson, who wrote *Damage Done: Suicide of an Only Son,* lost her son, David, to suicide; and Marjorie Antus, who wrote *My Daughter, Her Suicide, and God: A Memoir of Hope,* lost her daughter, Mary, to suicide. Patty and David were in their midtwenties; Mary was still a teen.

You cannot read these biographies and not have your heart ache for these three young people who died in this unfortunate manner. What these books describe in each case is a person who is very loveable, oversensitive, has a history of emotional struggles, and is in all likelihood suffering from a chemical imbalance. Hearing their stories should leave you more convinced than ever that no God worth worshiping could ever condemn any of these persons to exclusion from the family of life simply because of the manner of their deaths. Gabriel Marcel had an axiom that said: "To love someone is to say of that person, you at least will not die." That's solid Christian doctrine.

As Christians we believe that, as a community of believers, we make up the body of Christ along with all those who have died in faith before us. Part of that belief is that Christ has given us the power to bind and loose, which, among other things, means that our love for someone can hold that person inside our family, inside the community of grace, and inside heaven itself. In all three of these books, these mothers make it clear that this is exactly what they are doing. Their family, their circle of grace, their love, and their heaven includes their lost child. My heaven, too, includes these three young people, as should any true understanding of God, of grace, of love, and of the family of life.

That's a deep consolation, but it doesn't take away the pain. For a parent, the loss of a child to any kind of death leaves a wound that, this side of eternity, will find no healing. The death of one's child goes against nature; parents aren't supposed to bury their children. The death of any child is hard, but if that death comes by suicide, that pain is compounded. There's the frustration and anger that, unlike a death from a physical disease, this is unwarranted, unnecessary, and an act of betrayal in some way. And there's the endless second-guessing: How responsible am I for this? How should have I been more alert? Where was I negligent? Why wasn't I around at the crucial moment? Guilt and anger comingle with the grief.

But that isn't all. Beyond all of this, which is itself more than sufficient to break a person, lies the stigma attached to suicide. In the end, despite a better understanding of suicide and a more enlightened attitude toward it, there is still a social, moral, and religious stigma attached to it, which is equally true in both secular and religious circles. In the not-too-distant past, churches used to refuse to bury on blessed ground someone who died by suicide. The churches have changed their attitudes and their practice on this, but, truth be told, many people still struggle in their gut to accord a blessed, peaceful farewell to someone who has died by suicide. The stigma still remains. Someone who dies in this manner is still seen as somehow accursed, as dying outside the family of life and the circle of grace. There is, for most people, nothing consoling in their deaths.

As I have already suggested, the majority of suicides should be understood as death by a mortal illness: a deadly chemical imbalance, an emotional stroke, an emotional cancer, or an oversensitivity that strips someone of the resiliency needed to live. Here, however, I want to address more specifically the issue of the stigma attached to suicide.

It can be helpful to reflect upon the manner in which Jesus died. His death was clearly not a suicide, but it was similarly stigmatized. Crucifixion carried a stigma from every point of view: religious, moral, and social. A person dying in this way in ancient Rome was understood to be dying outside the mercy of God and outside the blessing and acceptance of the community. The families of those crucified carried a certain shame, and those who died by crucifixion were also buried apart, in grounds that then took on their own stigma. And it was understood that they were outside the mercy of God and of the community.

Jesus' death was clearly not a suicide, but it evoked a similar perception. The same stigma as we attach to suicide was also attached to the manner in which he died.

Does the Church Contradict This?

Suicide, understood in this way, is not the act of despair that it has too often been seen to be.

When I first began teaching and writing thus about suicide, I received a number of sympathetic letters, particularly from people who had personally lost loved ones to suicide. Conversely, a number of people wrote and challenged my view by quoting the *Catechism of the Catholic Church,* which states that "suicide contradicts the natural inclination of the human being to preserve and perpetuate his life" and is thus "gravely contrary to the just love of self." (*Catechism,* 2281)

What's to be said about this? Does the *Catechism of the Catholic Church* contradict what I said about suicide? Is suicide an act that is always "gravely contrary to the just love of self"? There is no simple answer to that question, because everything depends upon how we format the word "suicide." What does it mean "to die by suicide"? Does it always mean the same thing, or are there perhaps radically different things being referred to by one and the same phrase?

We could help ourselves, I submit, by making a distinction between something that we might aptly call "suicide" and something else that might more properly be called "killing oneself." What's the difference? In the former case ("suicide"), a wounded, oversensitive person is overpowered by chaos and falls fatally victim to an illness; while in the latter instance ("killing oneself"), an arrogant, pathological narcissist, acting in strength, refuses to submit to the commonalities of human existence. Not everyone who dies by his or her own hand dies for the same reason, not by a long shot.

We can speak of someone as "a victim of suicide." The terminology is natural and apt. In a "suicide" a person is taken out of this life against his or her will. Why do I say this? Because in fact most of the victims of suicide whom you and I have known fit that description. They were claimed by a disease that they didn't choose. The act that ended their lives was not a freely chosen one. It's truer to say that suicide was something they fell victim to than to say that it was something that they inflicted upon themselves. Most especially it was not an act of arrogance, strength, or pride on their part. Every victim of suicide whom I have known personally has been the very antithesis of the egoist, the narcissist, or the strong, overproud person who congenitally refuses to take his or her place in the humble, broken structure of things. It's always been the opposite. In every case that I have known, the victim of "suicide" has had problems precisely because she or he was too sensitive, too wounded, too raw, too bruised, or otherwise unable to find the resiliency needed to absorb some of life's harshness. In the end, they succumbed to a disease more than they actively did anything positively to harm themselves.

"Killing oneself," as distinct from falling victim to "suicide," is quite different. It's how a man like Hitler passes out of this life. Hitler was not a victim in any sense. By every indication, he killed himself. Killing oneself, in an instance such as his, is an act of "strength," an act that roots itself in a pride, an intellectual arrogance, and a pathological narcissism that, like Lucifer, sets itself before the schema of things and says: "I will not serve!"

It's in cases like these, but only in cases like these, that suicide fits what is condemned as morally deficient in the *Catechism of the Catholic Church.*

The Old Idea of Dying a "Happy Death"

I am a Roman Catholic priest who has been engaged in pastoral ministry for many decades. In the Catholic culture within which I grew up, we were taught to pray for a happy death. For many Catholics at the time, this was a standard petition within their daily prayer: "I pray for a happy death."

But how can one die happy? Isn't the death process itself excruciating? What about the pain involved in dying, in letting go of this life, in saying our last goodbyes? Can one die happy?

But the vision here, of course, was religious. A happy death meant that one died in good moral and religious circumstances. That meant that you didn't die in some morally compromised situation, you didn't die alienated from your church, you didn't die bitter or angry at your family, and, not least, you didn't die from suicide, drug or alcohol overdose, or engaged in some criminal activity.

The catechetical picture of a happy death most often was an anecdotal story of some person who grows up in a good Christian family; is an honest, faith-filled, chaste, churchgoing person; but for a period of time drifts from God, from churchgoing, and from observance of the commandments so that, at a point, he no longer thinks much about God, no longer goes to church, and no longer takes Christian morality seriously. But, shortly before his death, some chance circumstance becomes for him a moment of grace, and he repents of his laxity, his immorality, and his negligence of church practice, returns to church, makes a sincere confession, goes to Communion, and, shortly after, is struck down by a heart attack or an accident. But grace has done its work: After years of moral and religious drifting, he has returned to the fold and dies a happy death.

Indeed, we all know stories that fit that description; but, sadly, we also all know stories where this is not the case, where the opposite happens: where good people die in very unfortunate, sad, and tragic situations. We have all lost loved ones to suicide, alcoholism, and other ways of dying that are far from ideal. We also all know of people, good people, who have died in morally compromised situations or who died in bitterness, not able to let their hearts soften in forgiveness. Did they die unhappy deaths?

Admittedly they died in an unfortunate way, but a happy or unhappy death is not judged by whether death catches us on an up-bounce or a down-bounce. For every person that fits the picture of a happy death, as described above, where death catches us on an up-bounce, there are others whose lives were marked by honesty, goodness, and love, but who then had the misfortune of being struck down in moment of anger, in a moment of weakness, in a moment of depression, or who ended up dying from an addiction or suicide. Death caught them on a down-bounce. Did they die an unhappy death? Who is to judge?

What is a happy death? I like Ruth Burrows's description: Burrows, a Carmelite nun, shares the story of a fellow nun with whom she once lived. This sister, Burrows tells us, was a good-hearted, but weak, woman. She had entered a contemplative convent to pray, but she could never quite muster the discipline for the task. And so she lived for years in that state: good-hearted, but mediocre. Later in life, she was diagnosed with a terminal disease that frightened her enough so that she began to make new efforts at becoming what she was supposed to be her whole life, a woman of prayer. But a half century of bad habits is not so easily changed. Despite new resolutions, the woman never succeeded in turning her life around. She died in her weakness. But, Burrows asserts, she died a happy death. She died the death of a weak person, asking God to forgive her for a lifetime of weakness.

To die a happy death is to die in honesty, irrespective of whether the particular circumstances of our death look good religiously or not. Dying in right circumstances is, of course, a wonderful consolation to our families and loved ones, just as dying in sad circumstances can be heartbreaking for them. But dying in circumstances that don't look good, humanly or religiously, doesn't necessarily equate with an unhappy death. We die a happy death when we die in honesty, regardless of circumstance or weakness.

And this truth offers another challenge: The circumstances of someone's death, when those circumstances are sad or tragic, should not become a prism through which we then see that person's whole life. What this means is that if someone dies in a morally compromised situation, in a moment or season of weakness, away from his or her church, in bitterness, by suicide, or by an addiction, the goodness of that life and heart should not be judged by the circumstances of that death. Death caught that person on a down-bounce, which can make for a more guarded obituary, but not for a true judgment as to the goodness of his or her heart.

3
DESPAIR AS WEAKNESS
RATHER THAN SIN

☙

Classically, both in the world and in our churches, we have seen despair as the ultimate, unforgivable sin. The simple notion was that neither God, nor anyone else, can save you if you simply give up, despair, or make yourself impossible to reach. Most often in the popular mind this was applied to suicide. To die by your own hand was seen as despair, as putting yourself outside of God's mercy.

But understanding despair in this way is wrong and misguided, however sincere our intent. What's despair? How might it be understood?

The common dictionary definition invariably runs something like this: *Despair means to no longer have any hope or belief that a situation will improve or change.* The *Catechism of the Catholic Church,* which sees despair as a sin against the first commandment, defines it this way: "By despair, man ceases to hope for his personal salvation from God, for help in attaining it or for the forgiveness of his sins. Despair is contrary to God's goodness, to his justice—for the Lord is faithful to his promises—and to his mercy," (*Catechism,* 2091).

But there's something absolutely critical to be distinguished here: There are two reasons why someone might cease to hope for personal salvation from God and give up hope in having his or her sins forgiven. It can be that the person doubts the goodness and mercy of God, or—and I believe that this is normally the case—the person is too crushed, too weak, too broken inside, to believe that he or she is lovable and redeemable. But being so beaten and crushed in spirit so as to believe that nothing further can exist for you except pain and darkness is normally not an indication of sin but more a symptom of having been fatally victimized by circumstance, of having to undergo, in the poignant words of Fantine in *Les Miserables*, "storms that you cannot weather."

And before positing such a person outside of God's mercy, we need to ask ourselves: What kind of God would condemn a person who is so crushed by the circumstances of her life so as to be unable to believe that she is loveable? What kind of God would condemn someone for her brokenness? Such a God would certainly be utterly foreign to Jesus who incarnated and revealed God's love as being preferential for the weak, the crushed, the brokenhearted, for those despairing of mercy. To believe and teach that God withholds mercy from those who are most broken in spirit betrays a profound misunderstanding of the nature and mercy of God who sends Jesus into the world, not for the healthy, but for those who need a physician.

Likewise, this too betrays a profound misunderstanding of human nature and the human heart. Why would a person deem herself so unlovable that she voluntarily and hopelessly excludes herself from the circle of life? It can only be because of a deep, profound wound to the soul (which no doubt is not self-inflicted). Obviously, unless it is a case of some clinical illness, this person has been deeply wounded and has never had an experience of unconditional love or indeed of faithful human love. We are facile and naïve when, because we ourselves have been undeservedly loved, we cannot understand how someone else can be so crushed and broken so as to believe himself or herself to be, in essence, unlovable. To paraphrase a painful question in the song "The Rose": *Are love, and heaven, really only for the lucky and strong?* Our common understanding of despair, secular and religious, would seem to think so.

But nobody goes to hell out of weakness, out of a broken heart, out of a crushed spirit, out of the misfortune and unfairness of never having had the sense of being truly loved. Hell is for the strong, for those with a spirit so arrogant that it cannot be crushed or broken, and so is unable to surrender. Hell is never a bitter surprise waiting for a happy person, and neither is it the sad fulfillment of the expectation of someone who is too broken to believe that he or she is worthy to be part of the circle of life.

We owe it to God to be more empathic. We also owe this to those who are broken of heart and of spirit. What Jesus revealed in his life and in his death is that there's no place inside of tragedy, brokenness, sadness, or resignation into which God cannot and will not descend and breathe out peace.

God is all-understanding. That's why we're assured that "a bruised reed he will not break, and a smoldering wick he will not snuff out." You can bet your life on that. You can bet your faith on that. And you can also live in deeper empathy and deeper consolation because of that.

4

RECLAIMING THE MEMORY OF OUR LOVED ONE

❧

When talking about suicide, at least to those who are left behind when a loved one succumbs to this, the same themes must be emphasized over and over again. As Margaret Atwood puts it, sometimes something needs to be said and said until it doesn't need to be said anymore. What needs to be said over and over again about suicide? That, in most cases, suicide is a disease; that it takes people out of life against their will; that it is the emotional equivalent of a stroke, heart attack, or cancer; that people who fall victim to this disease, almost invariably, are very sensitive persons who end up for a myriad of reasons being too bruised to be touched; that those of us left behind should not spend a lot of time second-guessing, wondering whether we failed in some way; and, finally, that given God's mercy, the particular anatomy of suicide, and the sensitive souls of those who fall prey to it, we should not be unduly anxious about the eternal salvation of those who fall prey to it.

Prompted by a particularly moving book by Harvard psychiatrist Nancy Rappaport, *In Her Wake: A Child Psychiatrist Explores the Mystery of Her Mother's Suicide,* I would like to add another thing that needs to be said about suicide—namely, that it is incumbent on those of us who are left behind to work at redeeming the life and memory of a loved one who died by suicide. What's implied in this?

There is still a huge stigma surrounding suicide. For many reasons, we find it hard both to understand suicide and to come to peace with it. Obituaries rarely name it, opting instead for a euphemism of some kind to name the cause of death. Moreover, and more troubling, we, the ones left behind, tend to bury not only the one who dies by suicide but his or her memory as well. Scrapbooks and photos are excised, and there is forever a discreet hush around the cause of their deaths. Ultimately neither their deaths nor their persons are genuinely dealt with. There is no healthy closure, only a certain closing of the book, a cold closing, one that leaves a lot of business unfinished. This is unfortunate, a form of denial. We must work at redeeming the life and memory of our loved ones who have died by suicide.

This is what Nancy Rappaport does with the life and memory of her own mother, who died by suicide when Nancy was still a child. After her mother's suicide, Nancy lived, as do so many of us who have lost a loved one to suicide, with a haunting shadow surrounding her mother's death. And that shadow then colored everything else about her mother. It ricocheted backward so as to have the suicide too much define her mother's character, her integrity, and her love for those around her. A suicide that's botched in our understanding in effect does that; it functions like the antithesis of a canonization.

With this as a background, Rappaport sets off to make sense of her mother's suicide, to redeem her bond to her mother, and, in essence, to redeem her mother's memory in the wake of her suicide. Her effort mirrors that of novelist Mary Gordon, who in her book *Circling My Mother*, attempts to come to grips with her mother's Alzheimer's and her death. Gordon, like Rappaport, is trying to put a proper face on the diminishment and death of a loved one, redeeming the memory both for herself and for others. The difference is that, for most people, suicide trumps Alzheimer's in terms of stigma and loss.

Few things stigmatize someone's life and meaning as does a death by suicide, and so there is something truly redemptive in properly coming to grips with this kind of stigma. We must do for our loved ones what Nancy Rappaport did for her mother—namely, redeem their lives and their memory.

5
THE PAIN OF THE ONES LEFT BEHIND

&

Now I would like to share the feelings and reflections of a woman who recently lost her husband to suicide. The victim of suicide may be at peace in God's arms, but those left behind generally take a long, long time to make peace with this kind of death.

Here are her words:

My husband abandoned me and his daughters about a year ago. Without any warning signs, he left us to fend for ourselves. Yes, he had seemed stressed out and unhappy, but always insisted that everything was fine. One day he didn't come home from work. The next day his body was found. He had killed himself.

Despite being surrounded by loving family and friends, this reality was mine alone. The pain was excruciating, a pain that no one could share. The loneliness was beyond belief. A black weight settled into my being, a weight that suffocates and crushes. I seemed to live in an alternative reality, that of hell. I prayed to God incessantly for help. Help, help, help. I needed help. My husband had betrayed me massively. My daughters were fatherless. Words cannot convey the pain, despair, suffering I felt. I hurt badly. Anger seethed out of me. I was enveloped in a brutal, black place. My being was crushed, my heart shattered irrevocably, my soul in dire need. Send me help. I need help. Please, Lord, send me help.

"Rest in God," a friend advised in a sympathy card. I was desperate to do this. I prayed and prayed. Yet no breath of peace fell on me as I cried each night for help. Yes, friends brought meals over, they did yard work, they tried to be there for me. But no one could share my pain, my living hell. I tried to rest in God, yet the loneliness was too much for me.

I turned from God; the pain of his abandonment was too great. I stopped going to church. I stopped praying. I stopped caring. I considered casual sex, drugs, and drinking. Whatever. I was broken and damaged and didn't really care anymore. I was still in an alternative reality, still in hell. I didn't care.

I started feeling better. Subconsciously I was still desperate, on my knees, begging God for solace. Help, help, help. This prayer, this simple prayer, this desperate prayer, wove itself into my being. The times I let myself feel it, I would break down in utter despair.

I made it through the first year, but barely. On the one-year anniversary, I relived each excruciating minute, the horror of viewing his body, the unbelievable pain of comforting my wailing daughters whilst desperately needing comfort myself. I went to the chapel where the vigil had been held and sobbed myself sick. I relived my hatred, anger, guilt, abandonment, blackness, despair. My anger slowly dissipated into sadness. Deep, deep sadness. A sadness that continues to squeeze my heart, my soul, my being.

My husband was not created to die by his own hand. He was created in God's image, to become the person God meant him to be. Instead he murdered himself. This is so brutally wrong and skewed. I cannot wrap my mind around it.

My priest told me that sometimes God leads us to what we fear most, to show us we have nothing to fear. It's true that I don't fear death anymore. I saw clearly when I saw my husband's dead body that his spirit was no longer there. I know without a doubt that he is at peace. I just don't understand how I will ever come to my peace, at least in this world. I feel permanently disabled and damaged and sad.

I cry as I breathe deeply and try to trust. Guide me, guard me, O Lord my God.

Dealing with Loss

What can we say in the face of such deep loss, inconsolable grief, or unrequited obsessions?

As a graduate student in Louvain, I once posed that question to the renowned psychologist Antoine Vergote: "When you lose a loved one, either through death or because that person dies to you in some other way, what can you do? What can you say to help someone in that situation?"

His answer was cautious, words to this effect: "When someone is grieving a deep loss, there is a period of time when psychology finds itself rather helpless. The pain of death or the pain of losing a deep relationship can trigger a paralysis that is not easy to reach into and dissolve. Psychology admits its limits here. Sometimes I think that the poets and novelists are of more use in this than is psychology. But, even there, they can offer some insight, but I am not sure anyone can do much to take away the pain. There are some things in life before which we simply stand helpless."

That was, I believe, a wise and realistic answer. The death of a loved one, or even just the pain of an unrequited obsession, can bring us to our knees, literally, and, as the author of Lamentations says, leave us with no other option than to "put our mouths to the dust, and wait!" Sometimes, for a period of time, the pain of loss is so deep and obsessive that no clinic, no therapy, and no religious word of comfort can do much for us.

I remember, about thirty years ago, sitting with a friend who had, that day, been rejected by his girlfriend. He had proposed marriage to her and had received a clear and definitive refusal. He was shattered, utterly. For some days afterward he had trouble simply going through the motions of ordinary living, struggling to eat, to sleep, to work. A number of us took turns sitting with him, listening to his grief, trying to distract him by taking him to movies, without really having much effect in terms of drawing him out of his depression and obsession. Eventually, of course, he slowly began to emerge from the grip of that overconcentration and, still further down the road, was able to regain his freedom and resiliency. But there was a time during which we, his friends, could not do anything else for him other than to be with him.

What can anyone say to someone who is in the throes of a deep loss or in the grips of an unrequited emotional obsession? We have our stock expressions that are not without merit: Life must go on. Every morning will bring a new day, and eventually time will heal things. Remember, too, you are not alone; you have family and friends to lean on. Beyond that, you have faith. God will help you through this.

All of that is true, and important, but not particularly consoling or helpful during an overpowering period of grief. I remember writing a series of letters to a woman who had lost her husband to suicide and was totally shattered by that, believing that she would never experience happiness again. Time and time again I repeated the same lines to her: "This will get better—but not right now! Time will heal this, but its rhythm cannot be rushed. You will get better, but it will take time!"

Is there anything practical beyond this that we can offer someone who is in deep grief or in the grip of a bitter emotional obsession?

In 1936, when his sister, Marguerite-Marie, died, the great Jesuit priest and paleontologist Pierre Teilhard de Chardin wrote these words in a letter: "I feel that a great void has opened in my life—or rather in the world around me—a great void of which I shall become increasingly aware. . . . The only way of making life bearable again is to love and adore that which, beneath everything else, animates and directs it."

Antoine Vergote suggests that sometimes time, only time, can bring about healing, and that in the interim the only real option is to bear the unbearable, to try to get one foot in front of the next, stoically, with patience, holding our pain with as much dignity as we can muster, while waiting for time to eventually work its alchemy, knowing that nothing can short-circuit that process.

But Teilhard suggests there is something that can help make the unbearable bearable—namely, a more conscious, deliberate effort to love and to adore.

How do we do that? Not easily. But we do it when—despite our crippling obsessions, restlessness, frustration, bitterness, and anxiety— we let our generous and noble side be the deepest voice inside of both our sympathies and our actions. When we are driven to our knees by loss and frustration, the best, and only useful, thing we can do is to genuflect in helplessness before a God who can help us and to express our affection to anyone who can support us.

6
DYING INTO SAFE HANDS

෨

I t's hard to say something consoling in the face of death, even when the person who died lived a full life and died in the best of circumstances. It's especially hard when the one who's died is a young person, still in need of nurturing and care in this life, and when that young person dies in less-than-ideal circumstances.

As a priest, I have a number of times been asked to preside at the funeral of someone who died young, either as the result of illness, accident, or suicide. Such a funeral is always doubly sad. I remember one such funeral in particular.

A high-school student had died in a car accident. The church was overpacked with his grieving family, friends, and classmates. His mother, still a young woman herself, was in the front pew, heavy with grief about her loss, but clearly weighed down, too, with anxiety for her child. After all, he was still just a boy, partly still in need of someone to take care of him, still needing a mother. She sensed how dying so young, in effect, orphaned him.

There aren't many words that are helpful in a situation like this, but the few that we have say what needs to be said—even if on that day, when death is still so raw, they don't yet bring much emotional consolation. What's to be said in the face of a death like this? Simply that this young boy is now in more-loving, more-tender, gentler, and safer hands than ours, that there's a mother on the other side to receive him and give him the nurturing he still needs, just as there was one on this side when he was born. No one is born, except into a mother's arms. That's an image we need to keep before us in order to more healthily imagine death.

What, more precisely, is the image? Few images are as primal, and as tender, as that of a mother holding and cradling her newborn baby. Indeed, the words of the most-renowned Christmas carol of all time, "Silent Night," were inspired by precisely this image. Joseph Mohr, a young priest in Germany, had gone out to a cottage in the woods on the afternoon of Christmas Eve to baptize a newborn baby. As he left the cottage, the baby was asleep in its mother's lap. He was so taken with that image, with the depth and peace it incarnated, that, immediately upon returning to his rectory, he penned the famous lines of "Silent Night." His choir director, Franz Gruber, put some guitar chords to those words and froze them in our minds forever. The ultimate archetypal image of peace, safety, and security is that of a newborn sleeping in its mother's arms. Moreover, when a baby is born, it's not just the mother who's eager to hold and cradle it. Most everyone else is too.

Perhaps no image then is as apt, as powerful, as consoling, and as accurate in terms of picturing what happens to us when we die and awake to eternal life as is the image of a mother holding and cradling her newborn child. When we die, we die into the arms of God, and surely we're received with as much love, gentleness, and tenderness as we were received in the arms of our mothers at birth. Moreover, surely we are even safer there than we were when we were born here on earth. I suspect, too, that more than a few of the saints will be hovering around, wanting their chance to cuddle the new baby. And so it's okay if we die before we're ready, still in need of nurturing, still needing someone to help take care of us, still needing a mother. We're in safe, nurturing, gentle hands.

That can be deeply consoling because death renders every one of us an orphan, and daily there are people dying young, unexpectedly, less than fully ready, still in need of care themselves. All of us die still needing a mother. But we have the assurance of our faith that we will be born into safer and more nurturing hands than our own.

However, consoling as that may be, it doesn't take away the sting of losing a loved one to death. Nothing takes that away because nothing is meant to. Death is meant to indelibly scar our hearts because love is meant to wound us in that way. As the German theologian and pastor, Dietrich Bonhoeffer, a martyr of Nazi Germany, once put it: "Nothing can make up for the absence of someone we love. . . . It is nonsense to say that God fills the gap; God doesn't fill it, but on the contrary, God keeps it empty and so helps us keep alive our former communion with each other, even at the cost of pain. . . . The dearer and richer our memories, the more difficult the separation. But gratitude changes the pangs of memory into a tranquil joy. The beauties of the past are borne, not as a thorn in the flesh, but as a precious gift in themselves."

One sentence of consolation that I do often offer at a funeral is this one: He is now in hands safer than ours. She is now in hands much gentler than our own.

The truth of those words can be particularly consoling when the deceased is a young person, someone whom we feel still needs the hands of an earthly mother and father and whom we would want to trade places with because we feel that he or she is too young to have to leave us and go off in death, alone. That is also true in the case of someone who dies in a far-from-ideal manner, such as suicide or a senseless accident. Our unspoken fear is always that there should have been more time, that we should have done something more, been more vigilant, been more supportive, and we worry about a loved one departing this earth in so unfortunate a way. Finally, we have this same anxiety about someone who dies and has had a life that somehow never seemed to be free of extraordinary bad circumstance and frustration, and we wish we could have somehow done something to make things better. In each of these cases, nothing can be more consoling than to believe that our loved one is now in far safer and gentler hands than our own.

But is this simple wishful thinking, whistling in the dark to keep up our courage? Fudging God's justice to console ourselves?

Not if Jesus can be believed! Everything that Jesus reveals about God assures us that God's hands are much gentler and safer than our own. God is the father of the prodigal son and, as we see in that parable from the Gospels, God is more understanding and more compassionate to us than we are to ourselves. We see, too, in that parable how God does not wait for us to return and apologize after we stray and betray. Like the father who runs to meet his wayward son on the road, God runs out to meet us and doesn't ask for an apology. We see, too, in the stories just preceding the story of the prodigal son how God does not leave us on our own after we sin, to come to our senses and return repentantly to him. Rather he leaves the ninety-nine others and comes looking for us, anxious, longing, and ready to carry us home, in spite of our sin.

Jesus gives us the assurance that God does not give us just one chance, but seventy-seven times seven chances—infinite chances. We don't ruin our lives forever by making a mistake or even by making that mistake inexcusably again and again and again. Finally, in St. Paul's farewell message to us in his Letter to the Romans, he assures us that, even though we can't ever get our lives fully right, it doesn't matter, because in the end nothing, absolutely nothing, can separate us from God's love and forgiveness. We are, in this life and the next, in hands far safer and gentler than our own.

God is not a God of punishment, but a God of forgiveness. God is not a God who records our sins, but a God who washes them away. God is not a God who demands perfection from us, but a God who asks for a contrite heart when we can't measure up. God is not a God who gives us only one chance, but a God who gives us infinite chances. God is not a God who waits for us to come to our senses after we have fallen, but a God who comes searching for us, full of understanding and care. God is not a God who is calculating and parsimonious in his gifts, but a prodigal God who sows seeds everywhere without regard for waste or worthiness. God is not a God who is powerless before evil and death, but a God who can raise dead bodies to life and redeem what is evil and hopeless. God is not a God who is arbitrary and fickle, but a God who is utterly reliable in his promise and goodness. God is not a God who is dumb and unable to deal with our complexity, but a God who fashioned the depth of the universe and the deepest recesses of the human psyche.

Ultimately, God is not a God who cannot protect us, but a God in whose hands and in whose promise we are far safer than we are when we rely upon ourselves.

ABOUT PARACLETE PRESS

Who We Are

Paraclete Press is a publisher of books, recordings, and DVDs on Christian spirituality. Our publishing represents a full expression of Christian belief and practice—from Catholic to Evangelical, from Protestant to Orthodox.

We are the publishing arm of the Community of Jesus, an ecumenical monastic community in the Benedictine tradition. As such, we are uniquely positioned in the marketplace without connection to a large corporation and with informal relationships to many branches and denominations of faith.

What We Are Doing

Paraclete Press Books | Paraclete publishes books that show the richness and depth of what it means to be Christian. Although Benedictine spirituality is at the heart of who we are and all that we do, we publish books that reflect the Christian experience across many cultures, time periods, and houses of worship. We publish books that nourish the vibrant life of the church and its people.

We have several different series, including the bestselling Paraclete Essentials and Paraclete Giants series of classic texts in contemporary English; Voices from the Monastery—men and women monastics writing about living a spiritual life today; our award-winning Paraclete Poetry series as well as the Mount Tabor Books on the arts; bestselling gift books for children on the occasions of baptism and first communion; and the Active Prayer Series that brings creativity and liveliness to any life of prayer.

MOUNT TABOR BOOKS | Paraclete's newest series, Mount Tabor Books, focuses on the arts and literature as well as liturgical worship and spirituality, and was created in conjunction with the Mount Tabor Ecumenical Centre for Art and Spirituality in Barga, Italy.

PARACLETE RECORDINGS | From Gregorian chant to contemporary American choral works, our recordings celebrate the best of sacred choral music composed through the centuries that create a space for heaven and earth to intersect. Paraclete Recordings is the record label representing the internationally acclaimed choir Gloriæ Dei Cantores, praised for their "rapt and fathomless spiritual intensity" by *American Record Guide*; the Gloriæ Dei Cantores Schola, specializing in the study and performance of Gregorian chant; and the other instrumental artists of the Arts Empowering Life Foundation.

Paraclete Press is also privileged to be the exclusive North American distributor of the recordings of the Monastic Choir of St. Peter's Abbey in Solesmes, France, long considered to be a leading authority on Gregorian chant.

PARACLETE VIDEO | Our DVDs offer spiritual help, healing, and biblical guidance for a broad range of life issues including grief and loss, marriage, forgiveness, facing death, bullying, addictions, Alzheimer's, and spiritual formation.

Learn more about us at our website: www.paracletepress.com or phone us toll-free at 1.800.451.5006

SCAN
TO
READ
MORE